Unworldly Wind

Unworldly Wind

Larry Kimmel

café nietzsche press
windsor, ct

Unworldly Wind

café nietzsche press
an imprint of:
bottle rockets press
p.o. box 189
windsor, ct 06095
www.bottlerocketspress.com
bottlerockets_99@yahoo.com
see also:
http://www.winfredpress.com

No part of this book may be reproduced in any form or by any electronic or mechanical means including information storage and retrieval systems and without permission in writing from the publisher, except by a scholar or reviewer who may quote brief passages.

Cover Art: Pixabay
Cover Design: Larry Kimmel

Acknowledgment is made to the following publications where most of these poems first appeared, some in slightly different form: *Blue Unicorn; Bottle Rockets; The Christian Science Monitor; Concise Delight; Contemporary Haibun Online; Country Journal (Huntington, MA); Encore; Forms (by Anthropos Theophoras Review); Frogpond; Epos; Ink, Sweat & Tears; Loch Raven Review; The Lyric; Lynx; Pine Island Journal; Magnapoets; Modern Haibun & Tanka Prose; Modern Haiku; The Nisqually Delta Review; Raw NerVZ Haiku; Simply Haiku; Sketchbook; Stuffed Crocodile; Tobacco Road - Poet & Poem; Waiting for You to Speak; World Haiku Review.*

Unworldly Wind was original published as "Two Books: Branch after Branch and As Far As Thought Can Reach," by Winfred Press.

ISBN: 978-1-7327746-1-2

Copyright © 2007, 2019 by Larry Kimmel
All Rights Reserved.

To Robert Francis
&
Floyd McAuslan

CONTENTS

UNWORLDLY WIND

Taking Notice

Taking Notice after a Long Dark Night	1
Maple Keys	2
Jack-in-the-pulpit	3
Beech Trees & Legend	4
E.H. Shepard's Painting of Eeyore's Birthday	5
After Reading an Epic Fantasy	6
Paths that Crossed	7
The Weight of One Small Death	8
View from a North Window	9
Each Stone	10
November Gold	11
Feeding Chickadees in Winter	12
A Winter Canvas	13
Branch after Branch	14
I Step Out on My Porch Near Midnight	15
Crossing the Connecticut River	16
The Winter Woods	17
Spring Beauties	18
An Easter Morning	19

A Cup for All Seasons

A Cup Full of Seasons	23
Consider the Birds	26
Kinds of Posterity	27
So Soon	28
Summer Syllables	29
A Kitchen Fragrance	30
Catnip Tea	31
Home of the Brave	32
In Memoriam	33
Wooden Chain	34
Mystery	35
Rattlesnake	36
The Class Ring	37
October Elegy	38
Regret	40

UNWORLDLY WIND

Winter Cottage 43
Spring Woods 44
After the Spade 45
Irises 46
Strange Harvest 47
Bright Days 48
The Home Front 49
Herr Stein 50
Maybe 51
The Doe 52
Bar Harbor 53
October Morning 54
Two Willows 55
Winter Lightning 56
Beyond Reason 57
From Now On 58
Another Take on Saturday Morning 59

PEDAL POINT

Pedal Point 63

SEEKING THE HERMIT-SAGE

Once in a Parking Lot 73
Two Worlds 74
Red Squirrel 75
A Parable 76
For the Lone Bird 77
On a Hillside in Vermont 78
In Living Muscle 79
Rose in Window 80
Reflections 81
In the Eye of the Cockroach 82
Propriety 83
Picnic 84
To Not And Wish You Had 85
Of What Significance 86
Lights Across the River 87
The Chronicler 88
Seeking the Hermit-Sage 89
Visiting Poet 90

Unworldly Wind

TAKING NOTICE

Taking Notice after a Long Dark Night

The dew is not yet burned
from the orchard grass—

Crows range the open sky
on easy wings—

To the north,
a chain saw pitch-shifting
gnars a tune—

The forsythia is yellow, the lawn,
salt-crusted with Spring Beauties—

A wasp dangles by—

To the north,
a great conifer falls, sputtering
like firecrackers—

I raise my coffee mug, greet
the acrid bite—

How clear, how crisp the air!

Maple Keys

May caught us in a fall
of maple keys,

showered us with the sting
of pure potential,

rained down her dizzy burden
on our shoulders,

paving this quiet street
with small misfortunes.

Jack-in-the-pulpit

"You kids stop that now.
  You'll harm it sure"—the
Jack-in-the-pulpit by
  Gramma's back porch.
    ―――――

O so carefully we scrunched
  the upright Jack,
where he stood like a spike
  in his purple pulpit

'neath that lick of a canopy, only
  to hear his
scritch-scritch-scritch.
  That was his sermon,

you see, and how Jack, the preacher,
  ever survived our
curious fingers, our
  inquisitional thumbs

to evangelize another day,
  is a marvel indeed.

Beech Trees & Legend

On the lawn sprawling down from the second yellow mansion on Main Street, among the other ancient trees (almost a grove) are two venerable beech trees, with the gray and rumpled skins of veteran elephants.
        Too huge to hug,
                              too tall to tally,
we love them for their smooth, silvery look and for their long life. They put forth only a few leaves, high up, like the vestiges of a once significant garb. Now, ancient as wise men, prophets, seers, or hermit saints, they stand tall and are monuments unto their own selves.

. . .

Two carved their names, enclosed them in a heart,
And still their love grows deep by beechen art,
Though they've been twelve and twenty years apart.

E. H. Shepard's Painting of Eeyore's Birthday

This framed print reminding me
of childhood playgrounds,
this pastoral scene where
"Pooh and Piglet look on as
Eeyore tries to put the balloon into the jar,"
got stuck in time
and just in time for just
beyond the vanishing point
a threat to childhood brews,
like the foreboding presence of Mordor,
like storm clouds on the horizon
of a picnic.

After Reading an Epic Fantasy

Quite suddenly, full blown,
out of the chubby cheeks of an infant wind,
a leaf landed on a mud-puddle,
like a strange, crude vessel launched
on a fathomless café au lait sea.
It tacked eastward for seven ticks of time
then lost its course in a birthday candle blow.

Later, by the sun-shrunken mud-puddle
that had beached the curled brown leaf,
an ant swam a minuscule cove.
But it was a gigantic monster,
and I saw the horrific peril of yet another episode
in the epic from which I'd been excluded,
too huge to be viewed
even as a comprehensible god.

Paths that Crossed

Along my back porch bannister, teetering
with all the caution of an afternoon bibber,
he carries his barley body with hauteur
above the dust, on eight hair-thin stilts.

In the long, hot afternoon the mind meanders:
  "daddy longlegs (or harvestman if you prefer);
  race: arachnid; color: albino—"

Albino. The mind shouts. The word becomes
the generator and I
the electrical impulse lost
in the terrible circuits
of superstition.   (Will it be plus or minus?)

Nonetheless, with a child-learned deftness
I catch one silver wire and place this aberration,
this frosted transistor
teetering along like a mechanical toy,
on solid ground.

I let him go. I let him go but not
without a shudder and not
without note
in this, our long, dark chronicle, together.

The Weight of One Small Death

When I lifted the dead sparrow
from the lawn, it was light,
incredibly light: lighter
than a sheet of paper; lighter
than the bird alive; nearly lighter
than the weight in hand,
which was light – light
as the thought of a bird.

View from a North Window

For a moment, the sun
on a red barn, dying,
on dry fields still as a gold death-mask
warmed yellow only to the eye
beneath the winter-prophesying sky,
before night's shadow gathers the last straws
of afternoon to its scrawny breast;
the sun on a red barn, dying,
resurrects a lone child, playing.

Each Stone

What they left behind them
are the stone fences.

Each stone,
    now covered by a patina of lichen;
Each stone,
    grayish-green, here,
    in the clean November sunlight;
Each stone,
    once held between two palms.

These stone fences
are their Stonehenge
to us:
miles and miles of hand-felt care
falling back into time
through the clear November air.

November Gold

In the aging afternoon,
at the far edge of the lichen-hued pasture
on which the remnants of last night's
snow lie like tufts of cotton,
the bleak branches of old pear trees brighten,
on and off,
beneath the surfing clouds,
catch November gold
between the surfing clouds,
in the hoary snarl of their broken fingers,
while beyond the pasture and the trees,
fields the color of copper lighten,
on and off,
all as though attached
to some neon advertising apparatus,
quietly flashing the hopeless SOS
of an age,
soon to slip into the western horizon, forever.

Feeding Chickadees in Winter

Already accustomed to the procedure,
it isn't long till one
flutters down from the sky to clutch
the edge of my hand;

a moment more to twitch and eye
the seed in my palm, select
two or three, and flit away—

                —such delicate talons!

the sensation lingers, engendering
a tenuous ache
                —a millet of love.

A Winter Canvas

Dawn's white-gold fingers reach through winter's
heavy breath on trees and stretch
across the hush of thick, deep snow.

Overnight, yesterday's world
has been reduced to the merest suggestion
of a charcoal sketch.   White!   The world

has been ravished by white. The terrible white
of purity.

Branch after Branch

Slats of clear gold sunlight
and snow like fur on every branch
and every branch after branch after branch
as far as thought can reach . . .

I go to see if our road's been plowed.
The many small birds melt
before my boots and frosty breath.

Branch after branch, vast in its snowy hush,
the universe is as big as you think it is—

and maybe one or two trees more.

I Step Out on My Porch Near Midnight

Snow,
flecked by moon made mica.

Cold, windless air—even
the roar of the woods
is faint tonight;

And faint, too,
the creak
of my leather jacket—faint

As the rigging of a galleon
heard across the seas of time . . .

While overhead
Orion faintly flickers.

Crossing the Connecticut River

A day of rain
in February and
from the bridge
in Sunderland,
the river—

broad and flat
and grey
like gunmetal,
and in parts,
sheening—

the trim of trees
along both banks,
drab plum and
pigment of iron—

very lovely,
very steel,
like a lithograph
in some

old tome—tombed
for posterity.

The Winter Woods

What presences around the cabin pressed
my consciousness through
the ghostly night, that now

in the winter morning sunlight,
like hoary skeletons, tease
the eye? The dead and the dormant

all alike; but come the leafy season,
green by God, will separate the dead
from the living.

Spring Beauties

Each year I mark the stationary progress
made by a cluster of Spring Beauties,
that at a distance are a band
of some religious sect arrayed
in frail lavender gowns, leaning
southward into the nearly impenetrable grass on
an endless pilgrimage, remarkable
for being at once onward yet having
no apparent point of departure or arrival.
I look on, fascinated
by their adherence to a persistent paradox,
and also by what they are—
spring beauties – beautiful flowers.

An Easter Morning

I flung open
the window
one daffodil morning;

in came
the clamoring chimes,
tormenting,

with faulted
intervals,
some weary hymn—

quite suddenly
prodding
a childhood bruise.

A CUP FULL OF SEASONS

A Cup Full of Seasons

The cup
was a tin cup bearing
in bas-relief a cast
of five figures from
a nursery rhyme.

First Season
At breakfast on cold mornings
sitting by the oven
getting warm enough on one side
for both sides
and looking out the frosted window
over snow-laden hills
to hills ice-blue in the distance
and being cozy beside the oven
scorched on one side
still shivering on the left
I'd drink my dark brown Postum
hot from that Winter cup.

Second Season
Over the fresh plowed field
by the fence line
where trees grew
with barbed wire deep in their guts
and brush grew up through stones
picked and piled there
from years of spring-plowed fields

ending along the fence line
where the dying cherry tree loomed over
the budding dogwood
where the maple sap ran down
the elderberry spouts
to drip into buckets
that sat on stacks of stone
there I'd take a taste of sugar water
cold and sweet from that Spring tin cup.

Third Season
Down by the barn in summer
towards evening
big green flies caroused the manure pile
outside the small barn
that held some rats, an uncle's car
and standing big-eyed and docile
in the dusky stall the cow named Betsy
who allowed herself to be milked by Grammy
who sitting on a three-legged stool
in the dusky stall milked Betsy
amongst the fragrant hay and dung
the first squirts torrent sounding
in the hollow bucket
there amongst the dust of chaff and straw
I'd have a Summer cup
of animal warm and frothy milk.

Fourth Season
Up hollow
below the Mennonite Church
down the road a way by the creek
where we had fished
for chubs and minnows the summer long
in the shade of the giant oak
its red leaves falling now
down on the weathered building

blowing inside the weathered building
right there in autumn
with all the good smell of apples
ripe and bouncing up the clanking belt
spilling red from the clanking belt
tumbling down to the grinding
clattering machinery below
right there in autumn
I'd have an Autumn cup of cider
sweet and warm from that noisy press.

    The cup
    was a tin cup bearing
    in bas-relief a cast
    of five figures from
    a nursery rhyme.

Consider The Birds

While my grandfather repairs an old clock
at the kitchen table, I watch the chickadees
and bluejays flutter down from bare branches
to where a hand has tossed sunflower seeds

and millet on crusted snow. They flutter down
to scuffle with their brethren, who in turn
return to the tree, only to rebirth below.
The clock is ticking now. *'our ground time here*

will be brief,' Kumin, in a title, tells us.
The ground is earth, of course—the branches,
a make-shift heaven. But why this greed-fuss,
when there is feed enough for all? Oh! but

there is. There's feed enough. *'Look at the birds,'*
who feeds them? A hand? More than a hand, I think.

Posterity

I once found a butterfly whose wingspan was a good
three inches of untold colors—a butterfly like the paper
airplanes I used to decorate, then toss from the porch
to fly
        high over the dirt road below,
        and
        high over the field beyond;

                the field cropped by Betsy the cow;
                the field with spindly thistles
                        like scaled-down radio towers—

like those airplanes whose wings,
        wings crayon-ornamented or tablet-ruled;
        wings that cut the air, that razor-slit a slot to slip
through, beneath that strange sunlight peculiar to
August Sunday afternoons—

like those airplanes,
        —the butterfly, whose wings in death were fixed
for flight.

So Soon

Our neighbor bounces her baby on her knee.
I walk away thinking, `babies make us
realize how seldom we smile', thinking, `because
we are out of practice, happiness pains us',

recalling an afternoon at the homestead
when I was eleven, and my youngest aunt
swung her first-born in a canvas swing that
fit him like a clown's over-sized swimming

trunks. Cheerful little guy that he was, his
pure impetuous glee was infectious,
and though it couldn't have lasted long, still,
my face ached when I stopped smiling. So soon,

so young to ache. And here today?—nostalgia,
sentimentality, the rags of happiness.

Summer Syllables

Today I heard the season's first cicada,
what we call locust here, its level buzz
holding all the good past summers' data
in one long, sizzling syllable, as does

on languid days, a slammed screendoor tell
of flypapers, dusty roads, and the shade
of apple trees and porches - and the smell
of new cut hay, the taste of lemonade,

the whine of gnats, the scat of cat birds -
tell of swimming holes and baseball cards to trade,
of streams to fish and berries by the quart -
tell of swarming bees, of beans to shell,

of sleeping dogs and roses—tell, in short,
of all that was, in one sweet brief report!

A Kitchen Fragrance

A kitchen fragrance brings back the log-house on the hillside; morning crows from hill to wooded hill; the weathered barn; Betsy the cow; black raspberries in the upper pasture;

chicken pens by the creek, chickens that cackled and some that cooed like reeds; and Rookie, the khaki-colored dog; and dirt roads that passed through pastures of Queen Anne's lace and goldenrod;

Whip-poor-will Falls; the cider press, shadowed by a fiery oak; apple tree branches, pewter in winter, pink in spring; the party-line of twenty-five rings; the wood furnace of my first-grade classroom; daffodil Easters;

the returning crops; and Granma, who endured the seasons to the number of ninety-times-four.

Catnip Tea

When your mother sent for Granma,
it was *ring around the rosy* as rosy you lay
in bed between the twisted sheets, for
the sure notion of that grave gentleman

was yours. But after Granma came
and frisked you for flushes and fevers
and gave her prescription (which was a kind
of diagnosis and prognosis, as well),

gave her prescription in those two
familiar words—CATNIP TEA—you
ascertained you'd not be needing
a winding sheet; gleaned you'd be oki-dokie

real soon; fathomed you'd resurrect next day—
and you did.

Home Of The Brave

For three days Grandma's best milker frothed
at the mouth, then died—clearly poisoned. A year
later, old Mike Kovitch, with a skin full, said:
"It a shame about that cow, someday I tell you

Mister Mahler," and so we knew what we already
knew, and Grandpa spoke true when he told us
a desire to see justice done would only result in
something else dying or burning down, and all

Grandma had said to old Mama Kovitch was:
"Those aren't your cherries to pick," it being
Grandma's one cherry tree and she counting on
the crop for preserves, and old Mama Kovitch

had gone off mumbling: *"Me think this free
country,"* no different than any other time.

In Memoriam
John Ira Bowman 1884-1974

Aged ninety, he said to Milly, his daughter,
*"Something goes out of life when a man can't
plan his work the night before and see it
through tomorrow."* Later that year, shortly

after the untimely passing of a son-in-law,
he said, *"Milly, now there'll be someone
over there to meet me."* And that night
the last of the strokes took him, taking

a week to do so. I believe life to be
a continuum, and having experience
of others gone before me, why not him?
Sometimes I think a stern grandfather

(still the very image of a stoic) frowns down
on once-honed tools that I've let rust.

Wooden Chain

Found in an attic and given to me, years back,
this wooden chain of three links, holding
the shackle of a lantern-like cage, a cage
of four corner-bars that hold, in turn,

a wooden ball the size of a marble, on which you
can see the fly-eye faceted flatness of
the knife's work, yet perfectly round, and all
this marvel carved from a single piece of wood.

I ponder its pedigree, as no one remembers
who carved it, and ponder, too, how the works
of an artist live on, have a life of their own,
taking their chances about the same as any

progeny, and further ask why it is
that old half-known things so tease the mind?
———

clasping my dad's hand
as once he gripped his father's hand
whose hand had once . . .

Mystery

Up in the woods you'll find a mystery,
where the trees are lean and tall and well-spaced,
where cylindrical lengths of stone, no more
than six to seven inches on the average,

evidence a drilling for coal. You'll find these stones
hidden in russet leaves and fern, but more
than that, there are two furrows, sunken like
the graves in family cemeteries, and in

between the furrows, you'll find a stump too high
to let a truck pass over it, and surely
older than these fading wheel ruts. We thought
it rotted and tried to loosen it but found

it firmly rooted between the shallow tracks.
And there it stays, as sure as mystery must.

Rattlesnake

Three on the path ahead of him stepped over
it unawares, and he, likewise thinking it
a stick, was stepping over it when it
stirred—sliddered off the path into a clump

of brush near at hand. They, not wanting it
on the farm, took up sticks and beat the brush
(one from each of the four directions), till out
it came streaking straight for him, who always

ended this tale palpitating his shirt
with pinched fingers—miming the fear—saying:
*" ... and I'll tell you, I was one scared young
fellah that day—What?—O, we got'em*

*okay. I came down on 'im good 'n' hard.
He didnt last long after that, you betcha."*

The Class Ring

I hold in my hand a ring. Moxium High.
Class of '58. The initials my own.
Within weeks, I'd left it by a public sink.
Loss noted and steps retraced—both

immediate, but ... *c'est la vie*. Seven
years later it returned, having found
Its way to the alma mater with its
postal pedigree, some half-dozen

other Moxiums. A worthy scholarship,
the particulars of that seven year odyssey,
which remains mute within the zero of
this prodigal trinket of youth, inanimate

wanderer, whose encircled secret rests
upon my palm, yet forever beyond my grasp.

October Elegy

After the burial she walked with me,
Where tall trees, standing in a clear
Sunlight, cast strict shadows across
The drive—a woman just past fifty,
Elegant and gracious, lovely to see.

"You came all the way from Maine, they say.
You must have been very fond of Kurt,"
Meaning her brother, my uncle by marriage,
    and that was true.

A far hill seemed the reds and golds
Of an old tapestry kicked against
The horizon, while the branches near
At hand were clad in tatters, and one
Old oak in rags of penny-brown.

"You were just a boy when I left home."

That, too, was true, and true still,
The infatuation a boy once felt
For her—though now as mellow as
A bronze medallion smoothed by the wear
    of a quarter century.

She took my arm, her white-gloved hand
Around my sleeve, and we walked awhile
In silence. Her step was steady, stately,
Despite the cant of her narrow heels

On the cinder drive. And leaving the drive
We crossed a quilt of yellow leaves,
Dimly reflected in the branches
Overhead, and I was made
Momentarily giddy by
                    the lightness of its color.

And as we joined the others, she let
Go of my arm, saying, "I must
See Joan before I leave," meaning
My aunt, her sister-in-law, and smiling
A smile of October charm she left me.

All that was eighteen years ago,
And now I am her age then, and now
I do not think that I shall ever
See her again, and that, I allow,
Is as it should be, now as the reds
And golds of old tapestry
Return, once more, to distant hills—
                    the same but not the same.

Regret
Rosa Pearl Zimmerman Bowman 1884-1975

The log house, also, the homestead,
seemed smaller with the furniture gone.
And in the empty room that was once the kitchen,
there was a scrape mark, a crescent scar, worn
in the wide-plank floor
        " ... and all I can figure is,
Grammy must've, for years, dragged
her foot getting up from the table. She had
such bad arthritis, you recall,
and she could never sit still for a moment,
always doing for others ... "
                      And I did
recall, that and other things—

And if I could see her again ... if I
could see her again, I would not be impatient;
if I could see her.

UNWORLDLY WIND

Winter Cottage

Unworldly wind, and dark the midnight forest. So cold the branches click like antlers. Beyond that, not much to know.

in the black of nothing—
    phantom bucks
        battle

Spring Woods
_____

Skunk-cabbages that yesterday were green napkins folded to stand upright, now forge the bog, swarm the wooded hillside . . .

        across the path
        a snake
        too cold to care

_____

After the Spade
_____

Tossed and meant for the field, but hanging looped and
limp from an apple bough, the snake's carcass.

after the spade
three inches and the tongue
still flickering

_____

Irises

───────────────

ladies gathered for
a garden tea and gossip
irises in bloom

And in the summer breeze these now beige irises seem to nod and whisper, and if you listen closely—the faint rattle of tea cups.

───────────────

Strange Harvest

_____

His first day home on the farm, unscathed by combat, he loses an arm to the combine harvester.

> last night
> a sister's auburn hair
> this morning white

_____

Bright Days
_____

Bright days, hand-in-hand—what a friendship we had then! You said, "The river is shampooing its hair," and we played Pooh sticks from its bridge.

> that glint
> in the forest -
> where did it go?

_____

The Home Front
_____

A lone bumble bee patrols a hole in the ground. Kill it and soon there's another. How am I to finish painting the house?

war and the rumors
  of war - still the routine
    of bee and clover

_____

Herr Stein

———————————

I can still hear Herr Stein saying: " ... but it is a good F, in fact, if there was such a thing as an F+, that's what it would be."

        at the nursing home
        explaining myself
        to a puzzled man . . .

———————————

Maybe

No name on a deed; no retirement coming; as for steady work—forget it. Some think I live this carefree life. Maybe I do . . . maybe.

        on my palm
          this snowflake
            swiftly becoming . . .

The Doe
_____

As the headlights touch her, her legs fold to unfold on the far side of the fence where she isn't . . . having vanished into thin dusk . . .

        gone -
    but the wonder
  of blood and spirit
     remains

_____

Bar Harbor

October sunrise
looking out to sea
everything ship shape

And on the beach, overnight sculptures of stone, stacked
by unseen hands . . .

October Morning
_____

High and motionless, the hot-air balloon seems painted on the October sky. Its flame, the distant roar of a Chinese dragon.

> so vivid -
> her fresh
> tattoo

_____

Two Willows

_____

Like lavender weather on a blue-or-blush barometer, the chartreuse willow, in my neighbor's lawn, stands between two weathers.

>	yellow willows
>	 blown back
>	 bring Laura

_____

Winter Lightning

Revealed as being himself, I hate a favorite uncle for not quite being my childhood hero.

talking of old times
as dusk crowds the kitchen window
winter lightning

Beyond Reason

_____

On this one way street, where two slatterns grapple over what? the evening traffic circumvents, discreetly.

        a flash of thigh
           taunts
        beyond reason

_____

From Now On
_____

She sleeps beside me bathed in moonlight. Saw what I saw, know what I know. Great sex still, but no heart for lovemaking.

    is this it?
    an empty canoe
    on a river
    slow
    as from now on

_____

Another Take on Saturday Morning
───────────────

Would like to be dark-haired, handsome, lean as a hickory, famous, and have a sense of well being—all on the same day.

   greying at the temple
   and still "the poem"
   unwritten

───────────────

PEDAL POINT

This symbol ** is used where double-spaces fall on page breaks.

Pedal Point

───────────────

The road winds
                down
                          and
                                    down
                                                through
    russet, wet and tattered woodland,
Windshield wipers bow & scrape, bow & scrape,
And serpentine the creek thrashes in its skintight gulch, having
        swallowed a storm
            overnight
            overnight
Grand schemes mostly tarnish, yet yesterday's Ys needs but a rub
        and a holler—

"Hwæt!"
And back she comes, her spires, her domes, her watery bells
        (burnished bronze in an ever lavender evening)—
While this other, darkly perceived, darkly persists—this

        Dim of afternoon and snowfall-gray,
        Where in shadow of buttressed wall she comes,

Stands with me—mute—on the first stone step of three
Above a path that passes through winter-drifted hush
Of churchyard monuments, to cross a footbridge into
Wooded-darkness of winter woods beyond—
The small stream trickling under ice—
The silent snowflakes
                         falling
                                      falling . . .

I woke!, sad of a wish for what there never was—

                    . . .

Down-shifting now, trav'ling fast over yellow leaves pasted to wet
        macadam (roller coaster stuff),
The rain-dripping woods on either hand,
The lasting lavender dusk of dream on my mind, and on
        the radi-♪ *o-o-o sweet baby* ♪—voice you'd love
        to sleep with,
And I am 3 decades back in Elyria, where evenings once settled
        on amber fields, like dusky lingerie still warm . . .
Where at the ragged edge of town waited Tate's Tavern and the
        almost nights of certain unlikelihoods, never ending . . .

                    . . .

The russet woods; Elyria; the dusk of dream; the lost city of Ys
        . . . amber, violet, rust motifs,
And like a dark pedal point, the agonies my steadfast father
        suffered, that for all my acquiescence, metaphysical,
        I know not what to think,
The mind adverts!

But *o-o-o* that *radi-o* voice, that curl of blue smoke, and the years
        touch thumb and finger—
And there's Syd, the very picture of a black face in negative, come
        to front his band at Tate's that Halloween, laughed our
        collective asses off—

And what might my father have made of my nights at Tate's?, out
 of his steady life and pasture ways (I am uneasy that
  the dearly departed thumb our brains for lack of books),
And his faith and my faith, being what they are, the same end by
 means unreconcilably expressed

♪ ... *but o sweet baby* ... ♪

They don't mesh: his kingdom a hillside acre; my trek into
 the orchid night . . .
His last act, to match new stone work with old, and each old
 stone hand selected from Penn's sylvan legacy—
  I remember, was there,
4 years old with a joy buzzer in my guts, knowing it to be
 a borrowed truck that had got its differential hung up on
 a mossy ledge . . .
Then some 18 odd years later, me again,

*lone firefly pulsing through endless forest of unending night,
 ceaseless odyssey, epic eternal . . .*

And now, the bottom of Thompson Hill Road and the old
 palomino: pensive old guy; hammock-slung and yellowing
 like ivory; constant as any old friend;

♪ *ol' pal o' mío* ♪

With back, rain-stained; and tail, lank to his fetlocks; he grazes
 lightly, the green October grass.

. . .

Coming along the valley road, the radio now an irritant: I punch
 punch punch the station settings, give Frank the finger
 ('that's life'), and twist it off,
And looking up—see! that the Halloween flare of the great

    pasture maple has guttered out—last night's winds, no doubt,

      ♪ *don't let Satan fff it out, this little light of mine* ♪

Devil be damned!

I sing of a siren and a sunken city—

     . . . Ellingtonian tones, city by Hammett, with lone nocturnal saxophone, or Mr. Eliot's violet hour transposed to Johnstown, Pennsylvania . . .

The black and purple emery of a certain evening gathers over
    level clean-edged roof lines (grainy like a newsprint
    photo, if you look intently)
And me, a kid, aching for the imagined one night stands of an era
    gone, thinking the desolate streets I walk, a poetry, when
    over a café curtain—What?!
A barmaid intent on fixing a red red garter circling a round white
    thigh caught in a fishnet stocking, black; and me, a kid,
    taut and taunted, teased beyond reason . . .
That wonderful evening
    (barmaid, my ass)
That wonderful evening, so like that Ys-z city of perpetual purple
    twilight dreamed—but J'town, Steel Town, with its
    wine-stained sky . . .

        . . .

After 45 years in the mills, after 45 years a machinist, without
    the qualifying loss of a finger, so not a machinist after all,
    but still a hero, what the surgery did.
17 hours they labored and for what?
What Lugosi did to Karloff in "The Raven," 1935—though,
    in fact, a heinous accident enacted slow-motion on
    the surgeon's sterile plank, 1990.

**
Now further along the valley, I see, in pelting rain, a half-a-
 hundred Guernseys, munching as they mosey northward
 toward the wooded hillside, its reds and golds subdued in
 the pelting rain, and think, 'he would have smiled at such
 a sight.'

. . .

What the surgery did.
17 hours they labored, opened the head from behind the ear
 forward, like a book cover, read the malaise and scraped
 the bone clean of the fatal thought; the censorship done,
 'a closed book,' 'all sewed up,' leaving the knowledge of
 pain, unspeakable.
Yes. Unspeakable.
For a closed book doesn't speak, can't swallow, has a broken eye,
 the twisted face of a movie monster; but the mind clear,
 cognizant of the happened horror, and lucid to spell out
 home concerns on a clip board alphabet,
The least, the last I could do, draw him an alphabet large enough.

Inside my chest a scum bubble foul of grief swells, till one great
 'SOB' bursts, having taken me unawares, as has so often
 happened this past year . . .

Can't afford to think on it.
Even a philosophy large enough to contain all the trees of an
 endless forest that holds in its whispery green-dusk all
 mysteries, cannot, or has not as yet, informed me what to
 think—
Branch after branch after branch as far as thought can reach, the
 Universe is as big as you think it is, and trying to think it
 1 or 2 trees more, I think—
What if, lost, you came to a shack in the forest—found in
 the half-light beneath the leafy vaults where shone a
 beam of sunlight, a hermitage . . .

Found there, a hermit-sage. One like those marvelous saints
    of Ys—say, Guénolé, in all his ascetic excess

    (the brackish water; the few loaves twice
    a week, mixed with ashes; the praying right
    straight out for 7 hours, arms held level
    over gravity),

O wondrous excess set against such wickedness as Dahut,
    princess of the Mary-Morgan sort—

"But Hey!
I can sing of waters what washed a town away . . . "

    . . .

                                       JOHNSTOWN, MAY 31, 1889.
The approaching flood water was heard as a continuous
    thunder. My grandmother heard it.
Though only 5, remembered it.
Saw the second-story wall burst in as they clambered for the roof.

    It was a 40 foot wave that came on the town, that
    day. A rolling brow with a 'death mist' hanging over
    it. And before it, by a split second, a force of air
    knocking small frame structures flat. Now there's the
    grit of an American epic, having that needful national
    character of a people. 'Snatchy grabs' on the
    playground. Remember? A greed that grabbed a
    town away, complete, as a hand that scoops up
    marbles at the recess bell, or dice (after a bad throw
    for 'us'). And no one called to make an account. Yes,

I've all that in my veins, and Ys I know.

                      Can I do it?—

**
Sing

(in long alliterative lines of longing)
steeples and spires into being,
Whoop the warp of watery bells into being,
Call up towers and domes and castles,
From emerald waters till high over all,
Higher than the highest pinnacle of all,
Cry the pewter castle of the pagan princess,
Cry the Korrigans castle, grandeur against God
By the pagan princess, wild unruly Dahut—

Can I do it?

Say the several sylvan saints of Quimper,
Shout the sieges of Grandlon, and sorrows whisper,
Bellow the grief and speak the grievance,
Sing the polyphony of flaw and treachery
To the last speck of the splendor lost . . . ?

And still farther along the valley road, the all Summer summer-long baseball field in rain.

. . .

Last Spring, across this same faded field, a large smoke plume hooked and flowed up river, a river itself, turning quite blue as it thinned amid the hillside trees, of the winter rusted, rested woods . . .

Last Spring, on an apple bough, a fat-backed bird turned sideways—revealing his identity   and the next day two more of his kind eyed me from a crocus lawn. 'An infestation of robins!' I thought, and thought,

'He always saw the year's first robin' (though allowed as how that February robin had likely wintered over).

He could look down, anytime-anywhere, and find a four-leafed clover, it didn't take him long, and then it came to me

as it comes to me now, that I will always see the first
    Spring robin first, find the four-leafed clovers . . .
And now ahead of me, the town of Colrain nestled at the base
    of the mountain, with its old brick church: blue-roofed,
    white steeple aslant . . .

. . .

Was it just two years ago, Christmas, that we came early through
    the valley, the air clear and cold, and there at the
    mountain's base the little town of Colrain?
How still we saw thee, in the morning light,
With a kinked plume of smoke moveless over each and every red
    brick chimney (a greeting card picture if there ever was
    one),
And in the house beneath each smoke-?ed roof, Christmas, about
    to happen to each excited boy and girl, always anew since
    the advent of this unique event—
Then up the mountain we went on our way to a Boston
    Christmas, that winter morning, yes, two years ago—

. . .

Today, down-shifting to take the mountain (the windshield wipers
    bowing & scraping),
The subdued reds and golds of the mountain trees up and ahead,
My thoughts in shades of amber dusk, and dusk of dream;
        in shades of Ys, and lone nocturnal saxophones . . .
        amber, violet, bronze, or rouge motifs—
And underneath it all . . .

The grim incessant drone of a grave insistent tone

SEEKING THE HERMIT-SAGE

Once In A Parking Lot

> "... my stress lay on the incidents in the development
> of a soul: little else is worth study ..." ROBERT BROWNING

Talking in the parking lot across
from the library, where it is shaded
by tall maples, we hear this *chit-chit-chit*
and, wondering, we look up and see a squirrel

watching us from a high branch,
while rotating the nut he's gnawing at.
Seeing us see him, he stops his eating,
stops his busy little teeth, and stops

the *chit-chit-chit*. Silence. Eyes meet eyes.
Then ... he scampers to a higher branch—
and we? I don't remember what we said
or did that day, after the squirrel, or before

the squirrel. Recall only an incident
whose soul-value was its greater value.

Two Worlds

Here, in the afternoon, the forgotten
herb garden, the broken sundial,
seem timeless and content in ruin.
Over there, beyond the hedge,

lies a parking lot that seems
to thrive on agitation.
Two worlds, my love, two worlds a step
apart, knowing nothing of one

another. I brought you here to show
you something for which I haven't
words, hoping you might have the words,
yet here we stand, a step apart,

in silence. Well then, let's move on—
we mustn't linger here in doubt.

Red Squirrel

In summer sunlight the red squirrel scoots up
and down the apple tree, free from all concern,
while the cat watches from the window, and
I from behind the screendoor. Next he runs

along his highway through the greeny treetops,
his highway in the sky, his highway
invisible to me, once run   And now he
takes the shortcut home, leaving branches jostling,

where he's leapt from tree to leafy tree—not
suspecting all the eyes that tracked him. I
suspect we, too, live free of inhibitions
we might otherwise be feeling, if we but knew . . .

And now on ground he swirls
           around around
     and rounds the corner,
    like water
         down
        a
        drain
         .

A Parable

Now upon a time in the city park
three soap bubbles, iridescent and
ethereal, come to ride the afternoon.
One drops in a draft and is soon snagged on

a spiny bough. Another is struck (mid-journey)
by a wanton stick. But the third, a perfect
sphere, still hovers, reflecting in its glister
sun and sky and all the summer-loving lawn

and life below. But not for long. Comes a
westward wind, o, a mere suggestion of
the thing, but the bubble shimmers, shudders,
drifts away, fades on the city sky-scape,

thins and grays, till like a kiss bestowed
on air, it isn't, isn't anywhere.

For The Lone Bird

Having taken the awaited package from
the mail box, I look up and see behind
the winter window, my son's mute
enthusiasm. That he, in his long

and troubled isolation, can still be made
happy by so little, touches me. And I think
of the sorrows surely to come (sorrows I
cannot hope to help, who in my role

have helped to make them probable).
And seeing him, so brave and trusting,
behind that winter window, that silent
window, I feel something akin

to heartbreak, and my far-seeing eyes
brim for the lone bird over the endless sea.

On A Hillside In Vermont

We stopped our climb to breathe by a ledge
that jutted out of the hillside pasture,
and heard in the quiet air a sound, a
sustained *shh*—on and on, like a small

machinery, and then we saw, thick as an arm,
pouring from fissure into fissure, a loop,
a muscle in taupe casing redistributing
itself slowly, a live thing returning to

its source, a train showing between two tunnels
till its tapered caboose slipped-flashed by
leaving only stone and silence, and
a sense of not having seen the engineer—

or that which engineered, wrought spectacle
and wonder on a hillside in Vermont.

In Living Muscle

A taupe snake, thick as a firehose,
and like nothing I've ever seen
in Massachusetts, before or since,
was ejected from beneath the car

ahead of mine. It coiled and leapt
some three or more feet above
the asphalt. There was no time,
no way, to miss its writhing hop.

It must have leapt at least two
times before it was tumbled, with
a blunt thumping noise, beneath
my own car, and what I saw in

the rearview mirror
was anguish sculpted in living muscle.

Rose In Window

A small snow sprinkles down—dandruff
through scraggly trees—and dawn's gray
effusion grieves for lack of color,
lack of warmth, lack of leaves, for lack

of all, but also framed within
the window, a narrow stem, sprouting
up from an oboe vase to end
in a ruby explosion or

a scarlet napkin, unfolding.
Against the lack you are too
richly crimson, rose in the window.
You are a red, red torch in the midst

of a dim awakening—yes, rose you are
and are beyond all reason.

———

Nefertiti –
was there ever such a woman?
what I wouldn't give
to stand in her aura,
know what she thought of her world

Reflections

In the dark depth of the one clear
pane of nine, I saw her love gaze
on the back of me, and in that same clear
glass, looked her in the face—saw

her darkly, until she saw that I
watched her and turned those loving
eyes aside. And when I turned to
face her, in the here and now, I saw

nothing of this affection. O,
her loveliness was ever hers,
and her cheer was ever mine, but
we were never again so intimate

as when we met in that clear, black glass—
that dark,
              ethereal
                          otherworld.

———

        frost-starred window -
        I stare through my reflection
        into the moonlit orchard

In The Eye Of The Cockroach

The ballerina at the bar bends
within the eye of the cockroach.
She is dressed in black tights and leotard.
A shaft of sunlight from a curtained

window spotlights her gracefulness,
tangles in her walnut hair. Her eyes
are sage, and she is, perhaps,
a great beauty. Now she tilts

her strict spine and dips again, and one
blue vein, just beneath the dewy flesh
of an almond-colored breast, shows
in the eye of the cockroach—shows more dark

and terrible than a jungle river,
flowing back and back to the secret heart.

Propriety

In silhouette, the large, dark eye
of the girl from India seemed
not to belong to the face at all,
but rather like a great, black beetle

attached to blind porcelain
and, maybe, about to crawl—
and the luscious lashes of unusual length,
closed & opened, closed & opened,

suggesting a butterfly's pulsing wings
clipped to a black-eyed Susan, say—
and for one tingling moment, I felt
I would reach out and possess this exotic

creature, this exquisite Agassiz humbug
and might have, but for propriety.

Picnic

So that was that. I walked a little ways
away from her and looked out over the valley,
and seeing that the shadow of the hill
we stood on had begun to inch across

the fields below, I hunkered down to watch,
recalling how I once had hunkered down
to watch a puddle clear, that never cleared
in the given time of my impatience. But this time

a tiny tussle in the grass at my feet
caught my attention, and I studied the ant's
intent until it dawned on me that its
vocation was the only work, perhaps,

for which this world was meant—to somehow struggle
homeward homeward a crumb of nourishment.

To Not And Wish You Had

Think of it. Jenny Wade. The only
civilian causality of that three day battle
at Gettysburg, eighteen-sixty-three.
Killed in a kitchen while baking bread.

Killed by a bullet that strayed through the door,
which, as a lad, I saw, and the hole, too,
that the bullet made, enlarged and worn smooth
by all the fingers that had verified

the fact. I did not, myself, with finger, further
wear away the truth, for propriety's
own sake. (For we, I understood, were not
so common as to do as common does.)

But I wish I had. Still, to not and wish
you had, is also an experience.
———

        thirty long winters
        a misplaced fidelity
        still rankles

Of What Significance

For some years now, this phantom tableau, often seen.
A knight; a snowy field; a barberry bush,
its red berries bright above the snow, but
prickly to the eye without its leaves. The knight

on a palfrey beside the bush, and all environed
by clear air and hush of snow—an expanse
of snow bounded by a distant smudge. A smudge
which is forest. And like the forest, the middle-

distance vague, as well. Details adverting
from any tic to know, like peripheral
presences which will not be confronted with
a stare. Turn, and like that! they aren't. Unlike

the knight; the snowy field; the barberry bush;
and this—words without voice—this: "The Christ Child."

Lights Across The River

In summer you never thought a town
so close, not even when hearing shreds
of music wafted through the river's
jungle-voluptuous trim on clover

scented evenings; but now, as you
look far across this tiny tundra
of winter fields to where the distant
trees are stuck like antlers along

the river's edge, the lights beyond
are very near. Interesting
to think how in our time, oceans
have shrunk from months to hours, and yet

this unbridged abridged Amazon
still separates by half a year.

The Chronicler

Quill, scriptorium, ink of pokeberry,
a lasting stack of parchment. I see myself
in a tower overlooking a mountain pass,
with a ribbon of road below that follows

the twisting glint of a khaki river. A scant
traffic passes—carts, wagons, families on foot—
from which I deduce fires, famine, armies
out of control. A world in flux

or ended. Another not perceptibly begun—
begun, regardless, in this scripting now
of a past for what future? Have I brothers?
No matter. A lavender twilight enthralls me,

enchants this hour of my lonely work. I
am he who lives to scribe the chronicle.

Seeking The Hermit-Sage

I see myself on a mountain, an old man
loafing in sunlight, who long since came seeking
the hermit-sage, who not finding him,
lingered, among the pines, a night, a day,

another night and day, to this very hour.
Loafing, I finger the beads of incidents past:
recall the earth-cave found beneath an oak;
the foraged-food enough; and the learned-fire,

friend against winter; the rude hut built;
and the quieting of mind, which I compare
to the slow clearing of muddied water. And now,
on this ledge, as an old man reflecting, loafing

in sun-warmth, it simply comes to me that I
am he, found at last—the hermit-sage.

Visiting Poet

With a silent movie's flicker on an aster sky,
the starlings wheel St. Mary's spire, tilt,
so that, like Venetian blinds, you see less
of them. Later (after espresso at

The Rubáiyát), the ivy walls *screechscreech
screechscreech* like rusty cot springs. Can you see
even one among the leaves? And in
an alleyway of old brick walls, zapped

by lightning fire escapes, against a gust
of burger-scent and grime, I make a lantern
of my fist. Get grit in eye. Cigarette lit.
And see behind a dingy windowpane

one red geranium. And later still,
the clean-edged roofs against an orchid sky.

About the Author

Larry Kimmel was born in Johnstown, PA. He holds degrees from Oberlin Conservatory and Pittsburgh University, and has worked at everything from steel mills to libraries. He lives quietly in the hills of western Massachusetts.

To learn more about the work of Larry Kimmel see:
http://www.winfredpress.com

www.ingramcontent.com/pod-product-compliance
Lightning Source LLC
Chambersburg PA
CBHW060203050426
42446CB00013B/2970